THE CARIBBEAN
TODAY

CARIBBEAN ISLANDS
FACTS & FIGURES

Flags of the Caribbean

Anguilla

Antigua and Barbuda

The Bahamas

Barbados

British Virgin Islands

Cayman Islands

Cuba

Dominica

Dominican Republic

Grenada

Haiti

Jamaica

Montserrat

Netherlands Antilles

Puerto Rico

St. Kitts and Nevis

St. Lucia

St. Vincent and the Grenadines

Trinidad and Tobago

Turks and Caicos

U.S. Virgin Islands

THE CARIBBEAN TODAY

CARIBBEAN ISLANDS
FACTS & FIGURES

Wheaton Warrenville South High School
Library Learning Center
Wheaton, Illinois

Romel Hernandez

Mason Crest Publishers
Philadelphia

Produced by OTTN Publishing, Stockton, N.J.

Mason Crest Publishers
370 Reed Road
Broomall, PA 19008
www.masoncrest.com

First printing

1 3 5 7 9 8 6 4 2

Library of Congress Cataloging-in-Publication Data

Hernandez, Romel.
  The Caribbean islands : facts and figures / Romel Hernandez.
      p. cm. — (The Caribbean today)
   ISBN 978-1-4222-0622-5 (hardcover) — ISBN 978-1-4222-0689-8 (pbk.)
  1. West Indies—Juvenile literature. [1. West Indies.] I. Title.
  F1608.3.H47 2008
  972.9—dc22
                                        2008032767

THE CARIBBEAN
TODAY

Bahamas
Barbados
Cuba
Dominican Republic
Haiti

Caribbean Islands:
Facts & Figures

Jamaica
Leeward Islands
Puerto Rico
Trinidad & Tobago
Windward Islands

Table of Contents

Discovering the Caribbean

James D. Henderson

THE CARIBBEAN REGION is a lovely, ethnically diverse part of tropical America. It is at once a sea, rivaling the Mediterranean in size; and it is islands, dozens of them, stretching along the sea's northern and eastern edges. Waters of the Caribbean Sea bathe the eastern shores of Central America's seven nations, as well as those of the South American countries Colombia, Venezuela, and Guyana. The Caribbean islands rise, like a string of pearls, from its warm azure waters. Their sandy beaches, swaying palm trees, and balmy weather give them the aspect of tropical paradises, intoxicating places where time seems to stop.

But it is the people of the Caribbean region who make it a unique place. In their ethnic diversity they reflect their homeland's character as a crossroads of the world for more than five centuries. Africa's imprint is most visible in peoples of the Caribbean, but so too is that of Europe. South and East Asian strains enrich the Caribbean ethnic mosaic as well. Some islanders reveal traces of the region's first inhabitants, the Carib and Taino Indians, who flourished there when Columbus appeared among them in 1492.

Though its sparkling waters and inviting beaches beckon tourists from around the globe, the Caribbean islands provide a significant portion of the world's sugar, bananas, coffee, cacao, and natural fibers. They are strategically important also, for they guard the Panama Canal's eastern approaches.

The Caribbean possesses a cultural diversity rivaling the ethnic kaleido-scope that is its human population. Though its dominant culture is Latin American, defined by languages and customs bequeathed it by Spain and France, significant parts of the Caribbean bear the cultural imprint of

Sunset on the island of Trinidad.

Northwestern Europe: Denmark, the Netherlands, and most significantly, Britain.

So welcome to the Caribbean! These lavishly illustrated books survey the human and physical geography of the Caribbean, along with its economic and historical development. Geared to the needs of students and teachers, each of the eleven volumes in the series contains a glossary of terms, a chronology, and ideas for class reports. And each volume contains a recipe section featuring tasty, easy-to-prepare dishes popular in the countries dealt with. Each volume is indexed, and contains a bibliography featuring web sources for further information.

Whether old or young, readers of the eleven-volume series DISCOVERING THE CARIBBEAN will come away with a new appreciation of this tropical sea, its jewel-like islands, and its fascinating and friendly people!

(Opposite) Shadows over Havana, the capital of Cuba and the largest city in the Caribbean. (Right) The U.S. Virgin Islands.

1 The Land

THE CARIBBEAN SEA is home to thousands of large and small islands, which arc from Florida's tip to the coast of Venezuela. These islands are sometimes called the West Indies.

Cuba, the largest and most populous island in the Caribbean Sea, lies just 90 miles (145 kilometers) south of Key West, Florida. To Cuba's north are the Bahamas, comprising some 700 islands, and the Turks and Caicos Islands. To the southeast lie Jamaica and the island of Hispaniola, which is divided between the countries of Haiti on the west and the Dominican Republic on the east. Puerto Rico, a commonwealth of the United States, lies further east. Cuba, Jamaica, Hispaniola, and Puerto Rico make up the island group called the Greater Antilles, the largest islands of the Caribbean.

A collection of smaller islands curving to the southeast makes up the

Lesser Antilles. Beginning with the U.S. and British Virgin Islands, the chain continues with St. Eustatius, Saba, Anguilla, St. Martin/Sint Maarten, St. Barthélemy, St. Kitts and Nevis, Antigua and Barbuda, Montserrat, and Guadeloupe (these are known collectively as the Leeward Islands). To the south are Dominica, Martinique, St. Lucia, St. Vincent and the Grenadines, and Grenada (these are called the Windward Islands). Further south are Barbados, Trinidad and Tobago, and Aruba, Bonaire, and Curaçao (the ABC Islands), which sit off the coast of Venezuela.

Mountains and Beaches

Seventy million years ago, during the Cretaceous period, a set of volcanoes violently erupted from the sea floor and formed most of the Caribbean islands. But not all the islands are of volcanic origin. The Bahamas are coral reefs, for example, and Trinidad was connected to the South American mainland just 10,000 years ago.

Many of the islands are crossed by mountain ranges, the peaks of the volcanoes that formed the islands millions of years ago. Although it occurs rarely, these volcanoes are capable of becoming active and causing great damage. For example, an eruption on Montserrat in 1995 destroyed many homes and forced two-thirds of the island's population to leave. Dominica's rough terrain made it a challenge for Europeans to colonize, and as the most mountainous island in the region, it remains mostly undeveloped today.

The Dominican Republic is home to the Caribbean's highest and lowest points. Pico Duarte towers about 10,100 feet (3,080 meters), earning the mountain the nickname "Roof of the Caribbean." Lake Enriquillo lies 114 feet

Camuy Caverns in northwest Puerto Rico is the third-largest cave system in the Western Hemisphere. More than 10 miles (16 km) of this vast underground area have been explored and mapped. It is one of many popular tourist attractions in the Arecibo area.

(35 meters) below sea level.

The terrain across the region, even on a single island, can range widely, from rugged *rain forests* to rolling hills to dry *savannas*.

The Caribbean is most renowned for its beaches, which can range from powdery sand to rocky cliffs. Some countries have developed tourist resorts on their beaches; others have left their coasts relatively untouched, making them a destination for visitors who prefer natural beauty. The reefs surrounding some islands are popular spots for snorkeling and diving.

Fragile Wildlife

The Caribbean's wildlife is varied and colorful. Leatherback turtles cruise the warm waters off Cuba. Green monkeys cling to the treetops in

Barbados. A tiny tree frog called the *coquí* is Puerto Rico's national mascot.

The Caribbean is a bird-lover's paradise, and there are thousands of exotic species that can only be found on the islands. A bird-watcher might spot squawking macaws lounging in a rain forest, purple-throated hummingbirds flitting among flowers, or pink flamingos striding across a lagoon.

Unfortunately, many creatures are endangered by hunting and the destruction of natural habitats. Hawksbill turtles are hunted for their shells. The Puerto Rican parrot's habitat has been reduced by deforestation. Conservation groups are working to preserve these species, and others, from extinction.

Quick Facts: Geography of the Caribbean Islands

Location: Caribbean Sea and Atlantic Ocean, north and northeast of South America.

Terrain: varies with region; Cuba, Barbados, Aruba, Turks and Caicos, and British Virgin Islands mostly flat; most of the Windward and Leeward Islands have mountainous, volcanic interiors.

Climate: tropical or subtropical; most islands face rains and hurricanes between June/July to October/November.

Elevation extremes:
lowest point: Lake Enriquillo, Dominican Republic—114 feet (35 meters) below sea level
highest point: Pico Duarte, Dominican Republic—10,100 feet (3,080 meters)

Natural resources: nickel, bauxite, iron ore, fish, lobster, beaches and other attributes that draw tourists.

Natural hazards: Hurricanes, droughts, floods, occasional volcanoes, occasional earthquakes.

Source: CIA World Factbook 2008.

The warm waters of the Caribbean, and the variety of marine life that can be found there, make the islands popular among scuba divers.

Many animals that are commonplace on the Caribbean islands today—for example, cows, horses, and pigs—were introduced to the islands by European colonizers 500 years ago.

Sunshine and Storms

The Caribbean's tropical climate attracts visitors from around the world eager to soak up the sunshine. Average temperatures range from about 75°F to 90°F (23°C to 32°C). High humidity may make for sweaty conditions, but the cooling *trade winds*, which blow from the northeast, take the edge off the heat.

The region's rainy season lasts from May to October. This is also the hurricane season, a time when powerful storms lash the islands. With heavy rains and winds that may reach 160 miles (257 km) per hour, hurricanes can cause devastating damage to life and property when they hit land. A storm that swept through the Lesser Antilles in 1780 killed a record 22,000 people. About six hurricanes develop annually in the region, but most remain at sea and never reach the coast.

The ABC Islands enjoy vastly different weather; they lie outside of the hurricane path and are relatively dry. Aruba receives only about 17 inches (43 centimeters) of rainfall annually. This number differs greatly from Jamaica's 77 inches (196 cm) of rain per year.

Quick Facts:
Size of the Caribbean Islands

Total area: 90,027 square miles (233,170 sq km)
  Anguilla: 39 square miles (102 sq km)
  Antigua and Barbuda: 171 square miles (443 sq km)[1]
  Aruba: 75 square miles (193 sq km)
  The Bahamas: 5,382 square miles (13,940 sq km)
  Barbados: 166 square miles (431 sq km)
  British Virgin Islands: 59 square miles (153 sq km)
  Cayman Islands: 101 square miles (262 sq km)
  Cuba: 42,803 square miles (110,860 sq km)
  Dominica: 291 square miles (754 sq km)
  Dominican Republic: 18,814 square miles (48,730 sq km)
  Grenada: 133 square miles (344 sq km)
  Guadeloupe: 687 square miles (1,780 sq km)[2]
  Haiti: 10,714 square miles (27,750 sq km)
  Jamaica: 4,244 square miles (10,991 sq km)
  Martinique: 425 square miles (1,100 sq km)
  Montserrat: 39 square miles (102 sq km)
  Netherlands Antilles: 371 square miles (960 sq km)[3]
  Puerto Rico: 3,515 square miles (9,104 sq km)
  St. Kitts and Nevis: 101 square miles (261 sq km)[4]
  St. Lucia: 238 square miles (616 sq km)
  St. Vincent and the Grenadines: 150 square miles (389 sq km)
  Trinidad and Tobago: 1,980 square miles (5,128 sq km)
  Turks and Caicos Islands: 166 square miles (430 sq km)
  U.S. Virgin Islands: 136 square miles (352 sq km)

[1] Antigua 108 sq miles/280 sq km; Barbuda 62 sq miles/161 sq km
[2] includes St. Barthélemy, St. Martin
[3] includes Bonaire, Curaçao, Sint Maarten, Saba, and Sint Eustatius
[4] St. Kitts 65 sq miles/168 sq km; Nevis 36 sq miles/93 sq km
Source: CIA World Factbook 2008.

(Right) Christopher Columbus claims land in the New World for Spain, October 1492. Columbus's landing, and the eventual arrival of other explorers and settlers from Europe, would forever alter the future of the Caribbean. During the colonial period, Spain, France, Great Britain, and the Netherlands fought over many of the islands, such as St. Lucia (opposite).

2 History

THE POPULAR IMAGE of the Caribbean is of an island paradise, but the region's turbulent history has been marked by bloody conflicts and suffering. Even before Christopher Columbus arrived in 1492, the native Arawak and Carib tribes waged war. When the Europeans arrived in search of gold, they virtually exterminated all the native tribes on the islands within just a few decades. The Spanish, English, French, and Dutch who conquered the islands created a lasting cultural legacy, but they also brought disease and slavery.

In modern times, as some of the islands gained independence from their colonial masters, corrupt *dictators* took power. Many leaders exploited the people of their young nations. While political and economic conditions are improving, most of the Caribbean islands are still struggling to overcome a hard, painful history.

First Inhabitants

The Ciboney people who lived on Cuba and the Bahamas were probably the earliest inhabitants of the Caribbean. Archaeologists disagree on when they first settled the islands, but most put the date somewhere between 5000 and 1000 B.C.

The Amerindian tribe from South America known as the Arawaks (also called the Tainos or Lucayans) settled the islands in about A.D. 200. About 1,000 years later, the warlike Carib tribe migrated to the region and clashed with the peace-loving Arawaks, running them off many islands.

Still, the Arawaks were the most populous tribe in the Caribbean when Christopher Columbus arrived in 1492. They lived in independent villages headed by chieftains called *caciques*. The cassava root was a staple of their diet, but they also grew corn and hunted and fished. They worshipped gods called *zemis*. They painted their bodies in bright colors and wore gold and precious stones as jewelry. On several Caribbean islands, archaeologists have uncovered the remains of courts where Arawaks played a ceremonial ball-game similar to soccer.

The Caribs were fierce warriors who also moved to the Caribbean from South America. Armed with poison arrows, they painted their bodies red and traveled in canoes to launch raids on Arawakan villages.

There were fewer than a million *Amerindians* living on the Caribbean islands—the largest populations were on Cuba and Hispaniola (an island that today is divided into Haiti and the Dominican Republic)—by the time of Columbus's arrival.

A New World

Sailing under the Spanish flag, Columbus traveled in three small *caravels*—the *Niña*, *Pinta*, and *Santa María*—on a dangerous mission to find a westward route to Asia via the Atlantic Ocean. Instead, he "discovered" the Caribbean islands. On October 12, 1492, one of Columbus's sailors sighted land. Columbus named the island San Salvador—a part of the modern-day Bahamas. (Historians still disagree over exactly which island was San Salvador.) Columbus wrote in his journal, "The beauty of these islands surpasses that of any other as much as the day surpasses the night in splendor."

Two weeks later, Columbus sailed to Cuba and later to Hispaniola. He made a total of four voyages over the next decade, exploring many of the Caribbean islands, as well as the coast of South America.

The journeys of Columbus ushered in a wave of Spanish eager to discover adventure and gold. One of the first groups was led by Bartholomew Columbus—the explorer's brother—who founded Santo Domingo, the first permanent settlement in the Caribbean, in 1496. Although the *conquistadors* were at first friendly to the tribes they encountered, they soon made it clear they had come to take control.

Hatuey was a valiant leader of the Taino tribe who bravely fought the Spanish. He was captured in Cuba and sentenced to die. According to legend, when a priest asked if he wanted to convert to Christianity, Hatuey answered that he'd rather go to hell than a heaven filled with people as evil as the Spanish.

By the mid-1500s, the Arawak and Carib peoples had been practically wiped out by war and diseases, such as smallpox and measles, that were carried by the Europeans. The Indians had no resistance to these diseases, so they were often fatal. Today the Arawak are gone, but there remain a few scattered communities of Carib descendants throughout the region, most prominently on Dominica.

The Conquest

Spain was the dominant force in the Caribbean for more than a century. It established settlements on the islands and built forts to protect them from pirates and foreign invaders. The islands became important stopping points for galleons returning to Spain laden with gold and silver from Spanish colonies in Mexico, Panama, and Peru. In 1539 the Spanish built El Castillo San Felipe del Morro on a cliff above San Juan Bay in Puerto Rico, the eastern gateway to the region. The fort was the first line of defense for Spain against the waves of rivals who soon arrived.

Spain's exploration of the region opened the door to exploration from other European countries, especially England, France, and Holland. With the Amerindians mostly defeated, the countries battled for control of the strategic islands. Spain held tight to Cuba and Puerto Rico. France gained a foothold on Hispaniola. England took Jamaica. Holland grabbed some smaller islands.

In many cases, islands switched hands back and forth numerous times as countries invaded and counterattacked. Islands such as Tobago and St. Lucia changed possession more than a dozen times. Hispaniola was split between Spain and France, and St. Martin was shared by France and Holland.

Pirates such as the infamous Henry Morgan (1635–1688) and Edward "Blackbeard" Teach (1680–1718) roamed the seas, sometimes with the blessings of governments back in Europe, terrorizing settlers and smuggling goods. They established a rowdy haven in the Jamaican town of Port Royal, which was destroyed by an earthquake in the late 1600s.

The Europeans came to appreciate the value of the islands as more than just a way station. They established tobacco plantations on the islands, and by the 1600s sugarcane had become the major source of wealth. However, harvesting these crops required many men. The European powers turned to slaves from Africa to perform the grueling fieldwork.

As the New World prospered, so did the slave trade. Over 4 million slaves were captured, bound in chains, and brought to the islands; many more enslaved Africans died on the transatlantic journey. Once they arrived on the islands, the slaves were often treated brutally by their owners, who forced them to work extreme hours and to live in miserable conditions.

Blacks soon grew to be the largest racial group in the region, far outnumbering whites, and they remain so today. In Jamaica and some other islands, runaway slaves called *Maroons* established secret settlements in the island's rugged mountains and led revolts against plantation owners.

In 1834 Great Britain became the first colonial power to abolish slavery in the Caribbean. The other nations followed in later years—France in 1848, Holland in 1863, and Spain in the 1880s. However, for the most part blacks remained second-class citizens. It would be another century before blacks finally took hold of key government leadership positions in the Caribbean.

African slaves work on a Caribbean plantation in the 17th century.

After slavery was abolished, there was still a need for inexpensive labor. Some plantation owners brought *indentured laborers* from India and China to their islands. These workers were "indentured," or bound to harsh work contracts, but many stayed because there were greater opportunities available to them in the Caribbean than there were in their homelands. East Indians, as they are known, are the largest racial group in Trinidad and Tobago.

Struggles for Independence

A bloody slave rebellion in 1791 in Haiti (or Saint-Domingue, as it was known) against the ruling whites left more than 12,000 dead. The rebellion swelled to a full-blown revolution led by former slave Toussaint-Louverture (1743–1803). The French sent an army of 20,000 soldiers to stamp out the revolution, but the locals fought hard and Napoleon's forces retreated. Toussaint-Louverture, however, was captured and died in a French jail.

In 1804 Haiti became the first country in the Caribbean to declare its independence—the second country in the Americas to sever its colonial ties to Europe. (The first was the United States, which broke away from Great Britain in 1776.)

Throughout the 19th and 20th centuries, independence movements spread across the Caribbean—at times peacefully but often with turmoil and bloodshed. But independence did not necessarily mean that the people were any better off.

Haiti may have been the first Caribbean nation to gain independence, but in the two centuries since then the country has been plagued by political instability and a string of ruthless dictators. The U.S. military occupied the country from 1915 to 1934. François "Papa Doc" Duvalier (1907–1971) and his son Jean-Claude "Baby Doc" Duvalier ruled the country from 1957 to 1986. They used secret police to terrorize the people during their harsh regimes. In 1990 Jean-Bertrand Aristide was elected president but was overthrown within the year. Thousands of Haitians fled the island on makeshift rafts bound for Florida. With the backing of the U.S. military, Aristide returned to power in 1994 and won a second term as president in 2000. Haiti still struggles to overcome its internal disputes.

The Dominican Republic gained independence from Spain in 1844. The country endured dictators, civil war, and a U.S. military occupation before General Rafael Trujillo (1891–1961) seized power in 1930. Trujillo held office for three decades until he was assassinated. The

Toussaint-Louverture led a slave revolt on the island of Hispaniola during the late 18th century.

United States invaded the country again in 1965. The Dominican Republic finally became a democracy in the 1970s and has improved its living conditions, but it still suffers from political corruption, poverty, and crime.

In 1898 a mysterious explosion sank the battleship USS *Maine* in the harbor of Havana, Cuba. The United States blamed Spain, though that accusation has never been proven, and sent troops to aid an ongoing Cuban revolution against Spanish rule. After the war ended, the United States took possession of Puerto Rico and Spain agreed to grant Cuba independence.

As an independent nation, Cuba suffered under a long succession of mostly dishonest leaders backed by the U.S. government. In 1959 Fidel Castro led a revolution that later established a communist dictatorship on the island. The U.S. organized a failed invasion of the Bay of Pigs in 1961, then came to the brink of war with the Soviet Union in 1962 after the U.S. discovered nuclear missiles that had been delivered to the island.

During Castro's regime, the United States imposed an embargo on Cuba. Living conditions on the island grew worse after the collapse of the Soviet Union in the early 1990s. After nearly 50 years of political turmoil and hardship in Cuba, Fidel Castro stepped down as president in February 2008. His younger brother, Raúl Castro, was chosen to replace him as president.

The transition to independence and democracy ran more smoothly in most of the colonies of Britain, which planned ahead for each country's independence after the Second World War. The countries gradually assumed greater say over their affairs before they became independent, starting with Trinidad and Tobago and Jamaica in 1962. Montserrat and Anguilla have remained overseas territories of Britain.

The cannons of historic Fort George overlook modern cruise ships docked on the island of Grenada

Martinique and Guadeloupe remain part of France. Islanders elect a president but France appoints a prefect to oversee the governments. The citizens of Aruba and the Netherlands Antilles elect their own parliaments but maintain their ties to the Netherlands. The former French and Dutch colonies have enjoyed stability and are relatively prosperous compared with many of their neighbors.

What the Future Holds

The Caribbean faces new challenges as it moves into the future. Many countries are still working to diversify their economies. Cuba and Haiti, in particular, are suffering through economic depressions. AIDS is rampant on some islands. And of course natural disasters—hurricanes, earthquakes, or volcanic eruptions—could bring new hardships anywhere at any time.

If the past 500 years are any indication, the islands have proven that they can survive hard times and preserve the qualities that make them so distinctive.

(Opposite) Today, tourism is the major employer and source of revenue for many of the Caribbean Islands. This was not always the case, however. At one time agriculture, particularly the cultivation of such crops as sugarcane and tobacco, dominated the islands' economies. (Right) During the harvest on Barbados, a man carries sugarcane on his head.

3 The Economy

CHRISTOPHER COLUMBUS wandered into the Caribbean in 1492 intending to discover a new trade passage to Asia. He never found the route, but he opened a new world to exploration. Waves of greedy explorers dreaming of riches followed from Spain, France, England, Holland, and other European nations.

At first these hardy adventurers were lured by legends of gold, but they found little of the precious metal in the Caribbean. They instead used the islands as a jumping-off point to stage their violent conquests of South America.

In time the Caribbean offered up different riches. Today the islands are home to extremes—fabulous beach resorts and impoverished shantytowns.

27

Plantation Wealth

Spain encouraged development in the Caribbean by offering land to people willing to settle on the islands. These newcomers established large farms called plantations or estates. They forced the natives to work. After most of the natives were wiped out by disease and fighting by the mid-1500s, millions of Africans were brought across the ocean to work in the fields as slaves.

The first plantation owners exported what was for them a new plant—tobacco—as smoking became a popular trend throughout Europe. But by the 1600s, many of the island plantations shifted from cultivation of tobacco to sugarcane.

Over the past 500 years, some islands have developed thriving manufacturing industries and have promoted their cities and beaches as tourist destinations. But agriculture remains the economic backbone of the region. Many islands, from the Dominican Republic to Barbados, rely heavily on sugarcane exports. Martinique is a major exporter of bananas. Cigars made from Cuban tobacco are considered the finest in the world.

But agricultural economies are often unstable. The hurricanes that frequently sweep through the region can wipe out entire crops and crush a country's *economy*. Countries that rely heavily on a single crop can suffer when prices drop. When sugar prices declined worldwide during the 1980s, unemployment rates soared. Similarly, unemployment rose in Trinidad and Tobago when oil prices dropped in the mid-1980s. Many thousands of islanders fled for the U.S. and Europe in search of work.

Quick Facts: The Economy of the Caribbean Islands

Gross domestic product (GDP) is a measure of the value of goods and services produced within a country in a one-year period. It is often used as a measure of the size of a country's economy. Puerto Rico, for example, had the highest GDP among these Caribbean islands at over $77 billion in 2007. However, the size of an economy often depends on the population of a country—the more workers in the labor force, the greater the production should be and the higher the value of the goods produced. GDP per capita measures how the country's income is distributed, on average. The highest among the Caribbean nations in 2007 was Bermuda; although its 2007 GDP was $4.5 billion—less than 6 percent of Puerto Rico's—the GDP per capita of Bermuda was $69,900, significantly higher than Puerto Rico's $19,600.

Countries with a GDP per capita of $5,000 or less are considered low-income; those with a GDP per capita between $5,001 and $10,000 are considered middle-income countries. Countries with GDP per capita greater than $10,001 are considered to be fairly well-off.

The following chart provides a comparison of the gross domestic product and GDP per capita for the islands of the Caribbean.

Country	GDP	per capita	Country	GDP	per capita
Anguilla	$109 million	$8,800	Haiti	$11.14 billion	$1,300
Antigua and Barbuda	$1.53 billion	$18,300	Jamaica	$20.67 billion	$7,700
Aruba	$2.26 billion	$21,800	Montserrat	$29 million	$3,400
The Bahamas	$8.33 billion	$25,000	Netherlands Antilles	$2.8 billion	$16,000
Barbados	$5.32 billion	$19,300	Puerto Rico	$77.41 billion	$19,600
Bermuda	$4.5 billion	$69,900	St. Kitts and Nevis	$721 million	$13,900
British Virgin Islands	$853 million	$24,041	St. Lucia	$1.79 billion	$10,700
Cayman Islands	$1.94 billion	$43,800	St. Vincent/Gren.	$1.04 billion	$9,800
Cuba	$51.11 billion	$4,500	Trinidad and Tobago	$23.79 billion	$18,300
Dominica	$648 million	$9,000	Turks and Caicos	$216 million	$22,352
Dominican Republic	$61.79 billion	$7,000	U.S. Virgin Islands	$1.58 billion	$14,500
Grenada	$1.11 billion	$10,500			

Sources: CIA World Factbook, 2008

Several nations have banded together to form a partnership called the Caribbean Community and Common Market. Known as CARICOM, this organization promotes economic cooperation across the region.

Farms to Factories

The more prosperous countries in the Caribbean are those that have diversified their economies and ended their total reliance on agriculture.

After World War II ended in 1945, foreign investment helped to develop major industries in the Caribbean. This brought new wealth to many countries that were able to take advantage and expand their business opportunities.

Puerto Rico became a model for this new trend. The U.S. government offered tax breaks to companies, encouraging manufacturers of goods ranging from clothes to medicine to open factories on the island.

Trinidad and Tobago owes much of its relative prosperity to the discovery of oil. The country is the only one in the region with large oil reserves.

Mining is also important to several countries. Jamaica's major export is bauxite, a mineral used to make aluminum products such as cars and soda cans.

Cuba moved in a different economic direction from its neighbors. A revolution led by Fidel Castro established a communist economic system, under which the government took control of all business and private property. The United States strongly opposed the Cuban government's policies and announced an embargo, banning all trade with the island. Cuba grew to rely heavily on trade with the former Soviet Union and other communist nations.

The country struggled economically, and when the Soviet Union broke up in the 1990s, Cuba's economy crashed. Today many citizens find it difficult to get

Some cities in the Caribbean have become centers for international banking.

adequate food and medicine. The U.S. has refused to end its trade embargo until the government adopts political and social reforms and allows free elections.

Sun and Fun

The Caribbean's greatest natural resource may be its magnificent coasts. For years tourists have flocked to the islands for their gorgeous beaches and sunny weather. Cuba was for many years a playground for the wealthy. Prosperity in the United States during the 1950s helped to launch the tourism industry across the entire region as visitors headed south in search of surf and sand.

Most of the islands encourage tourism to some degree, relying mostly on the business of beach resort vacationers. Puerto Rico leads the region with over 5 million visitors annually. Relatively small countries such as the Bahamas and Aruba draw fewer visitors but depend on tourism dollars for more than half of their economy. The islands promote music and dance festivals; most countries hold an annual party in either winter or summer called Carnival. The colonial heritage of many countries, whether it's the Dutch influences on Aruba or the French flavor of Martinique, also makes the islands attractive to visitors.

Some of the smaller, less developed countries such as Dominica or Grenada have successfully encouraged eco-tourists who are more interested in exploring the rugged beauty of the islands than relaxing in swanky hotels.

Shady Deals

Some Caribbean countries are home to offshore banks, where the wealthy can hide money away and avoid paying taxes in their home countries.

The Cayman Islands, a British dependency, is home to over 40,000 banks with assets totaling $500 billion. Offshore banks bring the country wealth, which, along with further building up tourism, helps maintain one of the highest standards of living in the world.

In some cases, however, offshore banks may aid illegal activities by making it easy for criminals to stash away money in secret accounts.

Drug trafficking also has become a major business in the region. The islands are a major smuggling point for the cocaine and marijuana that are grown in South America and sold to buyers in the United States and Europe. Some countries such as Jamaica are major growers of marijuana.

In some cases government and military officials have been guilty of aiding traffickers. Most countries have joined U.S. efforts to fight drugs, but the illegal trade continues to flourish. Although the drug trade is illegal throughout the region, many people profit either directly or indirectly from the business.

Poverty in Paradise

Despite improvements over the past 50 years, many residents of the Caribbean live in desperately poor and miserable conditions.

Haiti is among the poorest countries in the world. Devastated by decades of political corruption and economic turmoil, about 80 percent of Haitians live in poverty. The country has the region's highest infant mortality rate and lowest life expectancy in the Caribbean. Nearly half the adult population can't read or write and at least one out of every four children suffers from malnutrition.

Even in Puerto Rico, which is part of the United States, or in such relatively well-off countries as Trinidad and Tobago there are huge gaps between the wealthiest and poorest citizens. In some cities such as Kingston, Jamaica, the wealthy dwell in marvelous hilltop houses above sprawling ghetto neighborhoods filled with rundown metal shacks.

The culture of the Caribbean islands is a mixture of influences—native, European, and African. Although millions of Africans were originally brought to the Caribbean as slaves in the 17th and 18th centuries, their descendants have made perhaps the most lasting contribution to the culture of the islands. (Right) Colorful costumes for a Carnival celebration.

4 The People and Their Culture

THE 40 MILLION people who dwell in the Caribbean can take pride in their rich cultural heritage, which often varies widely from one island to the next. Colonial-era influences are prevalent. The island languages include English, Spanish, and French, as well as unique *dialects* that incorporate African languages brought over by slaves hundreds of years ago. The African influence also has shaped the Caribbean's religions and forms of music and art.

While the Caribbean may be best known around the world for its beaches and sunny weather, its greatest strength is the great diversity of its people.

Arawaks and Caribs

Before Europeans arrived, the islands were inhabited for thousands of years by *indigenous* Amerindian tribes. By 1000 B.C. two groups predominat-

35

ed—the Arawaks and the Caribs. Today there are only a few scattered descendants of the Arawaks and Caribs, but islanders of all backgrounds take pride in their native roots. The native languages have stayed alive in scores of place names such as Haiti and Cuba and common words such as "hurricane" and "barbecue."

Dominica was one of the last Carib holdouts against European aggression and today remains home to more than 3,000 direct descendants of Carib Indians.

The Europeans

Caribbean exploration led to a massive scramble for land as the major powers of Europe fought for control of the islands. In many cases, possession of islands switched back and forth between Spain, Britain, France, and Holland. Today, many of the islands are independent nations, but the countries that once controlled them have left a powerful legacy that you can literally still hear on the streets. Haitians speak French, Cubans speak Spanish, Jamaicans English, and Arubans Dutch, but islanders have developed their own dialects. The inhabitants of the Netherlands Antilles speak Papiamento, a mix of Dutch, Spanish, and bits of African, Indian, and other tongues. Jamaicans and Haitians speak a blended version of English and French called Creole. Cuban Spanish differs greatly from the language spoken in Spain. Many Trinidadians of Indian backgrounds speak Hindi.

A single island may be home to vastly different cultures. Haiti, a former French colony, and the Dominican Republic, a former Spanish possession, share the island of Hispaniola. The island of St. Martin has a French side (St.

Martin) and a Dutch side (Sint Maarten), each with its own distinctive personality.

The colonial influence may be seen in many islands' historic **architecture**. The fine wrought-iron balconies of old buildings in San Juan, Puerto Rico, are unmistakably Spanish. The colorful gingerbread houses of Willemstad, Curaçao, are straight from Holland. The Anglican cathedral in Bridgetown, Barbados, dates back to the 1600s and illustrates why the island is still known as "Little England."

The Africans

After the Europeans virtually wiped out the native inhabitants, they turned to Africa for a new labor force. More than 4 million slaves were imported to work in the Caribbean between 1600 and 1870. Haiti, Jamaica, and Cuba took in the largest number—over 2 million combined, outnumbering whites. The workers were enslaved for life and horribly mistreated by their white masters.

African slaves and their descendants have made a profound mark on the culture of the islands, preserving to varying degrees their languages, religions, and music in unique ways that continue to enrich everyday life.

Blacks still make up the majority of island populations, from the Bahamas to Trinidad and Tobago. While whites have controlled the region's wealth and government for most of the past 500 years, blacks have made great inroads in the past 50 years. Among the great leaders were Trinidad and Tobago's Eric Williams (1911–1981) and Barbados's Grantley Adams (1898–1971). Both were charismatic and powerful figures who led their countries to independence and guided them for many years after. They are considered national heroes.

Religion

The European settlers established their religions—primarily Roman Catholicism and Anglicanism—when they settled the Caribbean. They forced slaves to convert to Christianity, but the slaves managed to keep alive their old religions. They adapted African gods and religious customs to Christian saints and rituals. This blended religion developed differently across the region: it is known as voodoo or vodun in Haiti, where it enjoys the strongest following, Santería in Cuba, and Shango in Trinidad and Tobago. Though the offshoots of the religion have evolved differently, all have origins in Africa.

Voodoo is the main religion of Haiti. Followers believe that there is a single god called Bondye, but there also exist family spirits known as *loa* who offer protection to the living. Priests act as intermediaries between the living and the *loa* and possess magical powers to heal, cast spells, and foretell the future.

Trinidad and Tobago is unique in the region for its large number of Hindus. Thousands of Indians were brought to work as indentured laborers after slavery ended. Hindu festivals such as Divali and Phagwa are major national holidays.

Literature

The Caribbean has produced many great poets and novelists, many of whom looked to the countries where they were born for creative inspiration.

Quick Facts: The Population of the Caribbean Islands

Anguilla: 14,108
Antigua and Barbuda: 84,522
Aruba: 101,541
The Bahamas: 307,451
Barbados: 289,968
Bermuda: 66,536
British Virgin Islands: 24,041
Cayman Islands: 47,862
Cuba: 11,423,952
Dominica: 72,514
Dominican Republic: 9,507,133
Grenada: 90,343

Haiti: 8,924,553
Jamaica: 2,804,332
Montserrat: 5,079
Netherlands Antilles: 225,369
Puerto Rico: 3,958,128
St. Kitts and Nevis: 39,817
St. Lucia: 159,585
St. Vincent/Grenadines: 118,432
Trinidad and Tobago: 1,047,366
Turks and Caicos: 22,352
U.S. Virgin Islands: 109,840

All figures are July 2008 estimates. Source: CIA World Factbook 2008.

Poets such as the Cuban José Martí (1853–1895), the Jamaican Claude McKay (1890–1948), and the Puerto Rican Julia de Burgos (1914–1953) all have written beautiful and haunting poetry about their respective countries. All were also active in politics—a tradition among Caribbean writers. Martí was a leader of Cuba's independence movements, McKay fought against racism, and de Burgos was active in her country's independence movement.

In recent years Caribbean literature has gained greater international acclaim. The poet Derek Walcott of St. Lucia and the novelist V. S. Naipaul of Trinidad and Tobago have won the Nobel Prize in literature, the most prestigious honor for a writer. Both Walcott and Naipaul have also written extensively about their countries.

Music

The Caribbean produces a range of musical styles, all great for dancing.

Salsa is most popular in Cuba and Puerto Rico. The style evolved from African musical traditions brought by slaves to the islands. A close relative of jazz, salsa is a spicy mix of percussion and beautiful melodies. Artists such as Cuba's Pérez Prado (1916–1989) and Puerto Rico's Tito Puente (1923–2000) helped to develop the salsa sound, which can be heard today in the music of pop entertainers like Ricky Martin, Jennifer Lopez, and Gloria Estefan.

Jamaica's musical export is reggae, a lively combination of African rhythms and rock music that developed in the 1960s. The lyrics of reggae songs often protest social injustices or describe life in the country's poor shantytowns. The greatest reggae performer was Bob Marley (1945–1981), who wrote classic hits such as "Stir It Up" and "I Shot the Sheriff."

Calypso developed in Trinidad and Tobago. Like salsa and reggae, the music has roots in Africa. The focus in calypso songs is on the lyrics, which often tell funny stories about romance and misadventure

Legendary reggae musician Bob Marley performs for a cheering crowd.

or satirize politicians. The steel drum, a musical instrument invented in the 1940s on Trinidad, often accompanies calypso singers. Steel drums are made out of empty oil barrels.

Sports

The warm and crystal-clear blue waters of the Caribbean make the islands a paradise for devotees of water sports such as sailing, diving, and fishing. But many natives turn to other activities for outdoor recreation.

In Cuba, Puerto Rico, and the Dominican Republic, baseball is the national pastime. Although all three countries have strong affiliations with Spain and its sports, American professional baseball also wields a strong influence. Some of today's greatest baseball players hail from these three countries. Players such as Juan Marichal of the Dominican Republic, Orlando Cepeda of Puerto Rico, and Tony Perez of Cuba are all members of baseball's elite Hall of Fame.

In countries with British connections, such as Barbados, Trinidad and Tobago, and Jamaica, most sports fans follow cricket. The game is played between two teams that take turns batting and bowling. Cricket has some similarities with baseball, though the rules of the British game are a little more complex. Although cricket is popular throughout all the countries that once made up the British Empire, the Caribbean has produced some of the sport's greatest players. Two legendary cricketers are Viv Richards of Antigua and Brian Lara of Trinidad. The best players from the islands play on the West Indies team, which competes with England, India, and Pakistan.

(Opposite) A small boat sails past office buildings in Port of Spain, the capital of Trinidad and Tobago.
(Right) A view of San Juan from the 16th-century Spanish fortress. San Juan is the capital of Puerto Rico; it is also the oldest city on the island, having been established in 1521.

5 The Cities

CUBA'S CAPITAL, HAVANA, is the largest city in the Caribbean—the romantic, bustling home of over 2 million people.

Havana was founded by Spain in 1514 as Batabano and five years later was relocated to its present-day site on the northwest coast. The city long thrived as the center of the Caribbean's booming sugar and tobacco trade, making it a frequent target of pirates and foreign invaders. The city's historic glory may still be glimpsed today in the Old Havana section, with its cobblestone streets and Spanish colonial architecture. Most of the area has become shabby and run-down in recent decades.

Havana serves as the seat of Cuba's communist government. Huge crowds swarm the Plaza of the Revolution to hear speeches by the country's government leaders. Havana is also the heart of the country's culture and nightlife, with museums, theaters, art galleries, and clubs like the Tropicana that put on extravagant shows.

Kingston, Jamaica

Home to nearly 700,000 Jamaicans, Kingston is located on a natural harbor surrounded by the Blue Mountains.

Kingston was founded in 1692 after nearby Port Royal, a notorious headquarters for the area's pirates, was destroyed in an earthquake. The city became the country's capital much later, in 1872.

Kingston is a city of both privilege and poverty. The city's waterfront is home to modern high-rises and expensive shops. But not far away are poor neighborhoods such as Trenchtown where people live in metal shacks.

Kingston is the Caribbean's largest English-speaking city, but many residents speak a Creole dialect that includes many African and Spanish words. The city is Jamaica's key port, where bauxite, sugar, and other exports are shipped out.

Santo Domingo, Dominican Republic

Santo Domingo, located on the southern coast of the Dominican Republic, holds the honor of being the oldest continuously occupied European settlement in the Americas. Christopher Columbus's brother Bartholomew founded the city in 1496. The colonial city section along the Ozama River preserves the buildings and atmosphere of the city's rich history.

There are more than 2.2 million residents in this sprawling capital city. Spanish is the most commonly spoken language. With its theaters, museums, and parks, Santo Domingo is a cultural center and major tourist destination. It is also a major port, exporting sugar, tobacco, and coffee.

San Juan, Puerto Rico

San Juan is Puerto Rico's largest and oldest city as well as its capital. With about 450,000 residents, this lively city is the country's center of banking and business. The local beaches also serve as a popular vacation destination for tourists seeking sun and nightlife.

Ponce de León (1460–1521) first settled Caparra, just west of present-day San Juan, in 1508. Thirteen years later, the Spanish moved to what is today the Old San Juan section of the city. The city's harbor grew into a jumping-off point for Spanish conquistadors exploring the New World.

Today, San Juan is a modern city with skyscrapers and fashionable resorts. The city's heritage is preserved in Old San Juan, a seven-square-block district of cobblestone streets and 400-year-old buildings and churches.

Port-au-Prince, Haiti

Port-au-Prince is Haiti's capital. The city and surrounding area are home to between 2.5 million and 3 million people. The city was settled by the French in 1749 and became the colonial capital in 1770. The residents speak Creole, a form of French that incorporates African languages.

Port-au-Prince is the country's cultural and economic center, home of the State University and the National Palace. But the majority of city residents suffer from poverty and live in violent, dilapidated shantytowns. As a result of years of economic and political upheaval, few tourists travel to the city.

Port of Spain, Trinidad and Tobago

Port of Spain is Trinidad and Tobago's capital. Located in Trinidad's northwest, the city is home to about 50,000 people. The city was founded by Spain in 1757 when the island's governor moved the colonial capital from St. Joseph. English is the most commonly spoken language.

Port of Spain is a cosmopolitan city with office towers and shopping malls alongside buildings that date back to the colonial era. It also serves as the island's busiest port, a stop for cargo and cruise ships alike. A major annual event is the winter Carnival, when thousands of extravagantly costumed revelers crowd the streets to dance to the rhythms of steel drums.

Nassau, the Bahamas

Nassau is the capital of the Bahamas. Located on New Providence Island near the Florida coast, the city is home to more than 210,000 people.

Nassau was founded by the British as Charles Town in 1666. During its early years, the city was a haven for Blackbeard and other infamous pirates.

The charming, upscale city is a major attraction for tourists, the country's major source of wealth. Nassau is also home to numerous offshore banks. The Junkanoo festival held in December presents an African twist on Christmas that is uniquely Bahamian.

Bridgetown, Barbados

A bustling port on Carlisle Bay, Bridgetown possesses a distinctly British feel from its pubs to its cricket grounds. The capital of Barbados even boasts a Trafalgar Square with a statue of the British naval hero Lord Horatio Nelson—just like the original square in London.

Bridgetown gets its name from a bridge that was probably built by the native Caribs over the Careenage, a small sea inlet. The city was a vital port for the island's thriving sugar industry in the 1700s.

The city is home to about 96,000 people. English is the official language, but Bajans, as islanders are called, speak their own mix of English and African languages.

Fort-de-France, Martinique

Martinique's capital of about 135,000 residents retains a Parisian feel with its narrow streets and cafés. French is also the country's official language.

The city is a busy port (the country is a major banana exporter) with a popular park called the Savane. A famous landmark is the Schoelcher Library, built in Paris in 1889, then dismantled and shipped to the island where it was painstakingly rebuilt a few years later.

Fort-de-France became the country's capital in 1902 after Mt. Pelée erupted, destroying the former capital, St. Pierre, in a few minutes.

A Calendar of Caribbean Festivals

Every Caribbean country sets its own calendar of holidays and festivals, but **Carnival** holds a special place on many islands.

Traditionally a Catholic celebration marking the beginning of the solemn season of Lent, Carnival was originally introduced to the Americas by Europeans. The African slaves of the region adopted the holiday and gave it a special twist.

Today's Carnival fuses Christian and African traditions with wild costumes and masks, parades, and music. The holiday takes place in February, climaxing on the Tuesday before Ash Wednesday, but some islands elect to hold Carnival in mid-summer.

January

Three Kings' Day on January 6 marks the visit of the Three Wise Men to the infant Jesus. Families exchange presents on this day, a bigger gift-giving holiday than Christmas in Latin American countries such as Puerto Rico and the Dominican Republic. Cubans celebrate the holiday, too, but the government's restrictions on religion have diminished its popularity on the island.

February

The **Anguilla Cultural Festival** highlights island life with arts, local music, food, storytelling, and crafts.

March

Trinidad and Tobago hosts the biggest, wildest **Carnival** in the Caribbean. The extravaganza in Port of Spain includes calypso bands and wandering minstrels. Traditional costumed characters derived from African legends such as Jab Jab the pitchfork-wielding devil, Moko Jumbie the stilt-walker, and Dame Lorraine the aristocratic lady mingle among the massive crowds.

Trinidadians begin festival preparations soon after the New Year, building up to the all-night party climax called J'Ouvert.

April

The yacht races of Antigua's **Sailing Week** attract sailors and sailing enthusiasts from around the world.

June

Turks and Caicos celebrates the **Queen's Birthday** in grand style. While commemorating the country's historical ties to Britain, the celebration also highlights island culture with parades, storytelling, and dancing.

July

The **Merengue Festival** in the Dominican Republic celebrates the country's joyous national music and dance. Top merengue artists entertain crowds that fill Santo Domingo to listen and dance to the music's bustling beat.

Guadeloupe's **Festival of Gwo Ka** centers around the traditional music style that originated with island slaves hundreds of years ago. As drummers improvise elaborate rhythms, singers and dancers respond with chants and songs.

A Calendar of Caribbean Festivals

August

Reggae Sunsplash in Ocho Rios and **Reggae Sumfest** in Montego Bay are rival festivals that highlight Jamaica's national music.

Two hundred years ago, slaves in Barbados started **Crop Over** as a celebration of the end of the sugar harvest. The festival died out along with the sugar economy until islanders revived the tradition in the 1970s. Today, Crop Over highlights island culture. The month-long celebration ends on Kadooment Day with a colorful parade and concert.

October

The Cayman Islands celebrate history during **Pirates Week**, a national festival that kicks off with a mock invasion of George Town Harbor by pirates in full costume. The festival celebrates the island's history as a notorious haven for pirates, drawing tourists with parades, concerts, and fireworks.

November

Haiti's **Fet Gede** (Feast of the Ancestors) takes place on November 2, All Souls' Day. A national holiday celebrating the island's voodoo religion and folklore, Fet Gede marks the new year. Port-au-Prince's cemeteries are filled with participants making offerings of coffee and rum to honor the dead.

Concordia Day, which takes place on March 23, commemorates the friendship between the Dutch and French inhabitants of Sint Maarten/St. Martin. The date marks the Dutch and French signing of a treaty dividing the island after years of conflict.

Divali, the Hindu Festival of Light, is a major holiday for Hindus on Trinidad and Tobago. A celebration of good triumphing over evil, celebrants light candles as offerings to Mother Lakshmi, the goddess of light.

December

Junkanoo, which is celebrated in the Bahamas, emerged from a period of rest that plantation owners gave their African slaves around Christmastime. Today the tradition continues as islanders hold competitions for the best-made costumes and headdresses.

Sint Nicolaas Day is a Dutch tradition kept alive on Aruba, Bonaire, and Curaçao. On the eve of December 6, Sint Nicolaas (a version of Santa Claus) arrives with candy and presents. Island children leave a bucket of water and a shoe filled with carrots and hay. The following morning, the children find the shoe filled with gifts.

Christians on the Caribbean islands celebrate **Christmas** on December 25.

Recipes

Pelau **(Trinidad and Tobago)**
2 cups rice
2 lbs chicken or beef, chopped into bite-size pieces
2 tbsp vegetable oil
1 tbsp soy sauce
Salt and pepper to taste
4-1/2 cups water
1 tbsp sugar
1/2 cup onions, finely chopped
1 clove garlic, finely chopped
1/2 cup celery stalks, finely chopped
1/2 cup tomatoes, chopped
1 green chili pepper, finely chopped
Mango chutney

Directions:
1. Season chicken with salt and pepper.
2. Heat oil in saucepan. Add sugar and heat until blackened.
3. Add chicken. Stir, cover, and cook over low hear for 10 minutes.
4. Add onions, celery, finely chopped garlic, tomatoes, and rice. Stir.
5. Add water, soy sauce, and whole pepper. Bring to a boil.
6. Cover and simmer for 40 minutes.
7. Serve with chutney.

Jerk Chicken (Jamaica)
1 tbsp. Allspice
1/2 tsp dried thyme
1/2 tsp paprika
1/4 tsp ground red pepper
1/4 tsp cinnamon
1/4 tsp garlic powder
1/4 tsp onion powder
1/4 tsp salt
1/2 tsp black pepper
1 tbsp soy sauce
Juice of 1 lime
2 lbs chicken drumsticks

Directions:
1. Mix all spices and soy sauce and lime juice in a bowl.
2. Add chicken and allow it to marinate overnight in refrigerator.
3. Grill chicken over hot barbecue or in broiler pan, turning regularly, for 45 minutes to an hour or until cooked through.

Black Beans (Cuba)
1/2 lb black beans, soaked overnight in water
1 large onion, finely chopped
1 large green bell pepper, finely chopped
4 garlic cloves, finely chopped
2 bay leaves
1/2 cup olive oil
Salt and pepper to taste

Directions:
1. Drain beans and place all ingredients in a saucepan.
2. Cover beans with fresh water and simmer for 1 hour until soupy.
3. Serve over cooked long-grain white rice.

Griot **(Haiti)**

2 lbs pork loin, chopped into 2-inch cubes
1 small onion, finely chopped
1 scotch bonnet chili, finely chopped
1/2 cup orange juice mixed with 1/2 cup lime juice
1/2 cup of vegetable oil
Salt and pepper

Directions:
1. Combine pork and other ingredients except oil in a bowl and marinate overnight.
2. Place pork in saucepan, add water to cover, and simmer over medium heat for 1 hour.
3. Heat oil in frying pan over medium-high heat and fry pork until browned.

Sancocho **(Dominican Republic)**
2 lbs chicken pieces
2 lbs yucca, peeled and chopped into small pieces
1 lb potatoes, peeled and chopped into small pieces
2 plantains, peeled and chopped into small pieces
3 large carrots, peeled and chopped into small pieces
1 medium onion, finely chopped
1/2 cup cilantro, finely chopped
5 cups chicken broth
3 ears corn, cut into quarters
Salt and pepper to taste

Directions:
1. Place all ingredients except for corn in pot, cover with broth, and bring to a boil. Simmer for 1 hour.
2. Add corn and simmer for 30 minutes.

Glossary

Amerindians—general term for the native people of the Americas; in the Caribbean, tribes include the Ciboney, Arawaks, and Caribs.

architecture—style of building construction.

caciques—village leaders of the Arawaks.

caravels—small sailing ships used by Spanish sailors in the 1400s and 1500s.

conquistadors—Spanish soldiers who colonized the Americas.

dialects—forms of spoken speech adapted from other formal languages.

dictators—leaders who rule with absolute power.

economy—a system of producing, distributing, and using goods and services.

indentured laborers—workers forced to work under strict contracts.

indigenous—native to a country or region, often referring to Amerindian tribes.

loa—spirits of the dead in the voodoo religion.

Maroons—runaway slaves who battled white plantation owners.

rain forests—dense tropical forests that enjoy heavy rainfall.

savannas—dry grasslands that receive seasonal rains.

trade winds—winds that blow steadily from the northeast to the equator, cooling the Caribbean.

voodoo—the magic religion of Haiti, derived from African religions; related to Santeria and Shango, other religions brought by slaves to the Caribbean.

zemis—gods of the Arawak religion.

Major Islands of the Caribbean: Maps

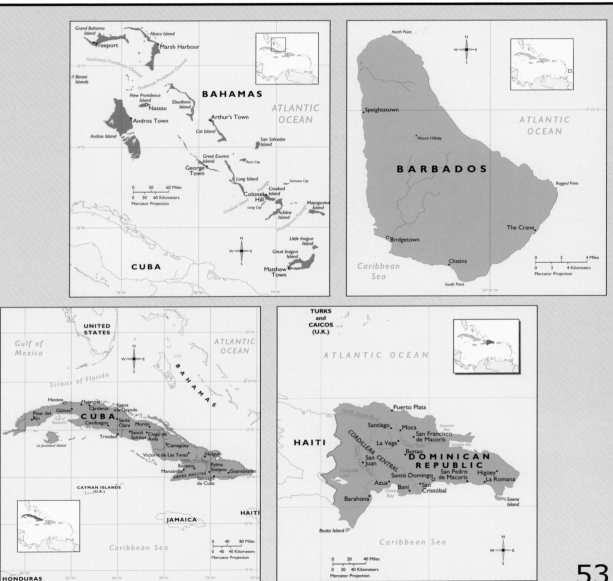

53

Major Islands of the Caribbean: Maps

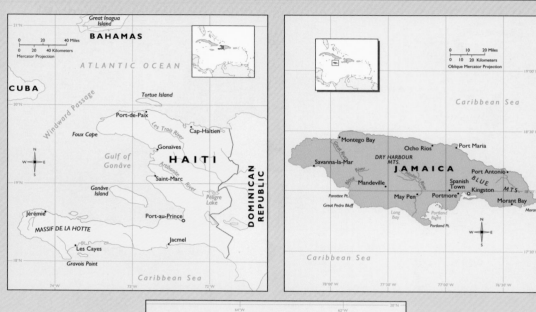

Major Islands of the Caribbean: Maps

Project and Report Ideas

A Biography Map

Write one-paragraph biographies of the following famous figures:

José Martí	Toussaint-Louverture
Bob Marley	V. S. Naipaul
Edward "Blackbeard" Teach	Tito Puente
Fidel Castro	Viv Richards
Eric Williams	Grantley Adams

Then draw a map that identifies the native lands of each of the famous people.

A Christopher Columbus Map

Using a map of the Caribbean, map the routes Christopher Columbus took on his four voyages to the Americas. Draw each of the routes in a different color, and in the map margins label the present-day names of the countries he visited.

Crafts

- Make color drawings of the national flags of three Caribbean countries and write short reports about the symbolism of the designs and their histories.
- For extra credit, design the flag of an imaginary country. Write a short report about the symbolic meanings of the flag's colors and design.
- Design and illustrate with your own drawings a travel brochure for a Caribbean country. Emphasize what might attract visitors to the island—its beaches, cities, wildlife.
- Make your own costume for a traditional Carnival character—Jab Jab, Dame Lorraine, Pierrot Grenade, and Fancy Indians are a few examples. Make sure to research how the character dresses and what his or her dress symbolizes.

Flash Cards

Break into teams, with each team creating flash cards of 10 common phrases from Jamaican Creole. Write the phrase on one side and its standard translation on the other. (Hint: there are several Creole dictionaries on the Web.) Teams can then compete to correctly define the opposing team's Creole phrases.

Project and Report Ideas

Reports

- Earthquakes, hurricanes, and volcanic eruptions all have caused extensive destruction and claimed many lives in the Caribbean. Choose one of these natural disasters and write an in-depth report based on your own research:
  1. For earthquakes, make sure to include information about faults and tectonic plates, the Richter scale, and safety measures to take when an earthquake strikes.
  2. For hurricanes, include information about the different stages of hurricanes, how they form and grow, and the famous storms that have occurred throughout history.
  3. For volcanoes, include information about the different types of volcanoes, why they erupt or become dormant, and famous eruptions that have occurred throughout history.
- Present an oral report about either the Arawaks or the Caribs. Research the tribe's history and way of life. What have archaeologists discovered about its culture?
- Write a first-person account of the life of a slave brought from Africa to work in the Caribbean. Do research about the slave trade and slavery in general to include authentic details about the voyage across the ocean and the daily life of a slave.

Chronology

before 1000 B.C.	The Ciboney tribe becomes the first group to inhabit the Caribbean islands. Historians disagree about when the tribe moved there; some believe they may have arrived as early as 5,000 B.C.
Ca. A.D. 200	Arawak Indians arrive from South America to settle the Caribbean islands.
Ca. 1000	Carib Indians move into the region, waging war against the Arawaks and occupying islands in the Lesser Antilles.
1492	On October 12, Christopher Columbus sights an island of the present-day Bahamas, names the land San Salvador, and continues on to Cuba.
1496	Spain establishes Santo Domingo on Hispaniola (present-day Dominican Republic), the first permanent European settlement in the New World.
1513	Spain authorizes the slave trade to import workers from Africa; over the next 250 years, over 4 million Africans are brought to the Caribbean.
1600s	Great Britain, France, and Holland fight with Spain and among themselves as they battle to expand their Caribbean empires.
1692	The pirate stronghold of Port Royal, Jamaica, is destroyed by an earthquake.
1780	A hurricane kills 22,000 people in the Lesser Antilles.
1804	Haiti declares independence from France after a long and bloody revolution.
1834	Great Britain becomes first European power to abolish slavery in its colonies.
1845	Indentured laborers from India begin to arrive in Trinidad.
1898	U.S. military intervenes in Cuban revolution against Spain; United States takes possession of Cuba temporarily and Puerto Rico permanently.
1902	Mount Pelée on Martinique erupts, killing 30,000.
1930s	The Great Depression devastates Caribbean economies.
1959	Fidel Castro leads successful revolution against Cuban dictator Fulgencio Batista.

1961	A West Indies Federation of British colonies fails; Rafael Trujillo, the Dominican Republic's leader for 30 years, is assassinated.
1962	Jamaica declares and gains its independence; Trinidad and Tobago declares and gains its independence; U.S. opposition to Soviet missiles on Cuba prompts the Cuban Missile Crisis, which almost leads to war before the Soviets agree to remove the missiles.
1983	U.S. invades Grenada to squelch political unrest.
1994	U.S. invades Haiti to reestablish rule of democratically elected president Jean-Bertrand Aristide; Hurricane Gordon kills 1,100 in Haiti.
1995	Montserrat volcano erupts, causing widespread destruction and evacuation of most islanders.
2000	U.S. and Cuba clash over fate of Elian González, a Cuban boy taken in by relatives in Florida; he eventually returns to Cuba and reunites with his family there.
2001	After years of protests, President George W. Bush agrees to phase out U.S. Navy operations on the Puerto Rican island of Vieques; tourism in Caribbean plummets after September 11 terrorist attacks on U.S.
2004	During the summer, a series of devastating hurricanes kill numerous people and cause millions of dollars worth of damages throughout the Caribbean Islands, particularly the Dominican Republic, Haiti, Jamaica, the Bahamas, Grenada, and Cuba.
2008	Representatives of CARICOM and the European Union discuss an economic partnership agreement that will lower tariffs on imports.

Further Reading/Internet Resources

Kurlansky, Mark. *A Continent of Islands: Searching for the Caribbean Destiny*. New York: Addison-Wesley Publishing Company, 1992.

Rogozinski, Jan. *A Brief History of the Caribbean*. New York: Penguin Putnam, 2000.

Scher, Philip. *Perspectives on the Caribbean: A Reader in Culture, History, and Representation*. Boston: Blackwell Publishing, 2008.

Scott, Caroline. *Insight Guide—Caribbean*. London: APA Productions, 2005.

Wilson, Samuel M. *The Indigenous People of the Caribbean*. Gainesville: University Press of Florida, 1999.

Travel Information

http://www.caribbeantravel.com
http://www.lonelyplanet.com/worldguide/caribbean
http://www.caribbean.com
http://travel.state.gov
  (Informaton about travel to Caribbean islands can be found here)

History and Geography

http://www.countryreports.org
  (Facts about all islands can be found here)
http://lanic.utexas.edu/subject/countries
http://memory.loc.gov/frd/cs/cxtoc.html

Economic and Political Information

https://www.cia.gov/library/publications/the-world-factbook/index.html
  (Facts about all islands can be found here)
http://www.caricom.org/

For More Information

Caribbean Tourism Organization
80 Broad St.
New York, NY 10004
Tel: 212-635-9530
Fax: 212-635-9511
Web site: http://www.onecaribbean.org
E-mail: ctony@caribtourism.com

Caribbean Community (CARICOM)
Secretariat
P.O. Box 10827
Georgetown, Guyana
Tel: 592-222-0001
Fax: 592-222-0171
Web site: http://www.caricom.org
E-mail: info@caricom.org

Institute of the Americas
10111 North Torrey Pines Rd.
La Jolla, CA 92037
Tel: 858-453-5560
Fax: 858-453-2165
Web site: http://www.iamericas.org

Organization of American States
17th Street & Constitution Ave., NW
Washington, DC 20006
Tel: 202-458-3000
Web site: http://www.oas.org
E-mail: svillagran@oas.org

Pan American Health Organization
525 23d St., NW
Washington, DC 20037
Tel: 202-974-3000
Web site: http://www.paho.org/

Summit of the Americas Center
Latin American and Caribbean Center
Florida International University
University Park, Miami, FL 33199
Tel: 305-348-2894
Fax: 305-348-1616
Web site:
    http://www.americasnet.net/democracy

Index

Index/Picture Credits

Page
2: © OTTN Publishing
3: Corbis Images
7: Corbis Images
8: Photo Disc
9: Corbis Images
11: Courtesy of the Puerto Rico Tourism Company
13: Corbis Images
16: Corbis Images
17: Hulton/Archive/Getty Images
22: Photos.com
23: Photos.com
25: Used under license from Shutterstock, Inc.
26: Corbis Images
27: Ted Spiegel/Corbis
31: Courtesy of the Curaçao Tourist Board
34: Corbis Images
35: Courtesy of the Curaçao Tourist Board
40: Hulton/Archive/Getty Images
42: Corbis Images
43: Photo Disc
53: © OTTN Publishing
54: © OTTN Publishing
55: © OTTN Publishing

Cover photos: Used under license from Shutterstock, Inc.

Contributors

Senior Consulting Editor **James D. Henderson** is professor of international studies at Coastal Carolina University. He is the author of *Conservative Thought in Twentieth Century Latin America: The Ideals of Laureano Gómez* (1988; Spanish edition *Las ideas de Laureano Gómez* published in 1985); *When Colombia Bled: A History of the Violence in Tolima* (1985; Spanish edition *Cuando Colombia se desangró, una historia de la Violencia en metrópoli y provincia*, 1984); and coauthor of *A Reference Guide to Latin American History* (2000) and *Ten Notable Women of Latin America* (1978).

Mr. Henderson earned a bachelor's degree in history from Centenary College of Louisiana, and a master's degree in history from the University of Arizona. He then spent three years in the Peace Corps, serving in Colombia, before earning his doctorate in Latin American history in 1972 at Texas Christian University.

Romel Hernandez is a freelance writer and editor based in Oregon. He was born in New Jersey and graduated from Yale. He is an award-winning daily newspaper journalist who has worked in New Jersey, Colorado, and Oregon. His other books include *Puerto Rico* in the series DISCOVERING THE CARIBBEAN.